W9-BYR-055

IT'S A CHAMELEON!

by Tessa Kenan

BUMBA BOOKS™

LERNER PUBLICATIONS ◆ MINNEAPOLIS

Note to Educators:

Throughout this book, you'll find critical thinking questions. These can be used to engage young readers in thinking critically about the topic and in using the text and photos to do so.

Copyright © 2017 by Lerner Publishing Group, Inc.

All rights reserved. International copyright secured. No part of this book may be reproduced, stored in a retrieval system, or transmitted in any form or by any means—electronic, mechanical, photocopying, recording, or otherwise—without the prior written permission of Lerner Publishing Group, Inc., except for the inclusion of brief quotations in an acknowledged review.

Lerner Publications Company
A division of Lerner Publishing Group, Inc.
241 First Avenue North
Minneapolis, MN 55401 USA

For reading levels and more information, look up this title at www.lernerbooks.com.

Library of Congress Cataloging-in-Publication Data

Names: Kenan, Tessa, author.
Title: It's a chameleon! / by Tessa Kenan.
Other titles: It is a chameleon!
Description: Minneapolis : Lerner Publications, [2017] | Series: Bumba books. Rain forest animals | Audience: Ages 4–8. | Audience: K to grade 3. | Includes bibliographical references and index.
Identifiers: LCCN 2016018696 (print) | LCCN 2016025862 (ebook) | ISBN 9781512425680 (lb : alk. paper) | ISBN 9781512429329 (pb : alk. paper) | ISBN 9781512427585 (eb pdf)
Subjects: LCSH: Chameleons—Juvenile literature. | Rain forest animals—Juvenile literature.
Classification: LCC QL666.L23 K46 2017 (print) | LCC QL666.L23 (ebook) | DDC 597.95/6—dc23

LC record available at https://lccn.loc.gov/2016018696

Manufactured in the United States of America
1 – VP – 12/31/16

Expand learning beyond the printed book. Download free, complementary educational resources for this book from our website, www.lernerresource.com.

Table of Contents

Chameleons Change Color

Chameleons are reptiles.

There are many kinds

of chameleons.

Most of them live in rain forests.

Chameleons are

different sizes.

Some are as big as a

pet cat.

Others are smaller than

your thumbnail.

Chameleons have

strong toes.

They have long tails too.

These help them hold on

to branches.

Chameleon eyes can look two ways at once.

Their big eyes look for food.

Why might it be helpful to look two ways at once?

A chameleon eats insects.

It shoots out its

long tongue.

The tongue is sticky.

It catches the insect.

Chameleons can change the color of their skin.

This chameleon turns red.

The red color tells other chameleons to go away.

Why might chameleons turn other colors?

15

Mother chameleons can

change color too.

This mother will lay

her eggs.

There can be one hundred eggs!

Why do you think chameleons lay so many eggs?

16

Then the mother goes away.

But the babies know what to do.

They can change color and catch

insects just after hatching.

Chameleons live alone.

They can live to be

twelve years old.

Parts of a Chameleon

eye

skin

toes

tail

Picture Glossary

hatching

coming out
of an egg

insects

small animals with
wings, six legs, and
three main body parts

**rain
forests**

thick, tropical
forests where
lots of rain falls

reptiles

cold-blooded
animals that
slither on their
bellies or walk
on short legs

23

Index

Read More

Carr, Aaron. *Chameleon.* New York: AV2 by Weigl, 2016.

Hansen, Grace. *Chameleons.* Minneapolis: Abdo Kids, 2015.

Raum, Elizabeth. *Chameleons.* Mankato, MN: Amicus High Interest, 2015.

Photo Credits

The images in this book are used with the permission of: © Cathy Keifer/Shutterstock.com, pp. 5, 23 (bottom right); © Dennis van de Water/Shutterstock.com, pp. 6–7; © David Havel/Shutterstock.com, pp. 8–9, 17; © Kuttelvaserova Stuchelova/Shutterstock.com, p. 10; © Francois Loubser/Shutterstock.com, pp. 12–13; © Iarus/Shutterstock.com, p. 14; © Nick Henn/Shutterstock.com, pp. 18, 23 (top left); © Darkdiamond67/Shutterstock.com, pp. 20–21; © Lipowski Milan/Shutterstock.com, p. 22; © Nadezda Zavitaeva/Shutterstock.com, p. 23 (bottom left); © encikAn/Shutterstock.com, p. 23 (top right).

Front Cover: © Kuttelvaserova Stuchelova/Shutterstock.com.